NLP

Commence The Process Of Comprehending The NLP Language And The Fundamental Role Played By Neuro Linguistic Programming In The Art Of Persuasion

Calvin Harper

TABLE OF CONTENT

What is NLP?..1

Convictions, Principles, Dispositions, and Conduct...22

Why is NLP Good For You?........................34

Restructuring: Ingenuity or evasion of reality? 43

NLP Techniques 52

Neuro-Linguistic Programming in Therapeutic Practice 86

Strategic planning for facilitating extraordinary life transformations.................................. 120

What is the correlation between depression and NLP? 142

What is NLP?

The prevailing issue faced by many individuals presently is their perception of being trapped or unable to progress. They hold the belief that regardless of their efforts, they would inevitably exemplify a predisposition towards tardiness in their professional commitments, an inability to meet deadlines, and a tendency to yield to any conceivable temptation that crosses their path. They are of the opinion that they are unable to control it.

It is plausible that you have experienced or are experiencing similar emotions at some juncture in your life. Should you choose to do so, it is possible that this inclination stems from the belief shared by individuals who struggle with making positive transformations - namely, that their disposition is inherently wired in this manner. To some extent, your perspective is accurate – every individual on this planet possesses inherent programming that elicits distinct responses to various circumstances. An instance of this is when you instinctively press the snooze button upon the activation of the alarm, despite your conscious awareness that you must rise early in order to avert a succession of familiar calamities such as tardiness at the workplace, subsequently leading to reprimand from your supervisor.

Please be advised that there is a positive development to be shared - a feasible approach exists for modifying the functioning of your brain, resulting in a lasting transformation within a relatively brief timeframe. Utilizing neurolinguistics programming, commonly referred to as NLP, can assist in attaining the desired behavioral outcomes.

NLP Defined

NLP is comprised of three major components, specifically neurology, linguistics, and programming. The neurological system serves as the orchestrator of your physiological processes, and language dictates the means by which you may engage in interpersonal communication and social interaction. Your programming determines the manner in which your mind and language interface, consequently influencing your overall conduct. One's conduct ultimately molds the reality they inhabit, as it is shaped by their demeanor and convictions.

NLP, viewed through the lens of a theoretical framework, can be characterized as a practical and results-oriented methodology. This system has been devised by Richard Bandler and John Grinder, in an endeavor to comprehend the underlying reasons why certain individuals are able to demonstrate exceptional competencies in tackling tasks that others might perceive as exceedingly challenging. In their comprehensive series of investigations, they unearthed a remarkable revelation pertaining to individuals: humans possess the capability to adeptly adhere to diverse models that serve as cognitive frameworks. Individuals also possess the capacity to reinterpret circumstances, which consequently enables certain individuals to distort or amplify the occurrences they undergo.

Gaining Insights into the Depths of Your Psyche

As an individual undergoes the process of maturation and encounters diverse life experiences, their cognitive faculties gradually establish neural connections that correspond to the knowledge and skills they have acquired. Upon consistently adhering to the choice of brewing a pot of coffee as your initial task in the morning, a segment of your cerebral faculties undergoes transformation, thereby facilitating the execution of said activity without necessitating a conscious evaluation of whether or not a cup is desired. Contrarily, the brewing process is carried out automatically upon your arrival at the pantry at the onset of the morning.

A considerable number of the activities you engage in adhere to this procedure. If, despite your advanced age, you continue to experience fear while sleeping in the absence of light, it is likely due to a process of neural adaptation in your brain that reinforces and amplifies your apprehension during nighttime hours. Other individuals who expeditiously overcome this unfounded apprehension have fostered their cognitive faculties in a different manner. These factors collectively signify that the development of the brain predominantly influences the abilities and limitations one may possess.

The choice of language employed greatly influences one's ability to effectively communicate both with oneself and others, subsequently shaping one's behavioral patterns. NLP acknowledges the presence of an individual's internal dialogue, and acknowledges that the manner in which individuals communicate with themselves influences their attitude.

By successfully altering the manner in which one engages in self-communication, it becomes possible to modify one's thought processes as well.

Fundamental Presuppositions

"NLP abides by these two premises regarding individuals:

1. The manner in which you are programmed is not unequivocal.

Individuals can exclusively comprehend reality based on their personal perceptual capacities, and their individual neurolinguistic frameworks function as the foundational guide by which they navigate their assorted encounters. Nevertheless, it should not be inferred that the world possesses the restrictions you perceive. By altering the cognitive framework through which you conceptualize the world, you would attain the ability to perceive alternate realities, modify your convictions, and access potential prospects that may be inaccessible through a prior mode of thought.

2. Your personal experiences and thought patterns can undergo diverse evolutions.

NLP asserts that, although an individual may have been conditioned to think or behave in a particular manner, numerous avenues for transformative change remain available to them. This indicates that the development of your personality and beliefs is not fixed or immutable. Rather, as you engage with others and navigate the experiences that come your way, your mind undergoes continual reorganization. All of your experiences have been meticulously orchestrated to yield the most optimal equilibrium.

Sub-modalities

By employing the methodologies and approaches of sub-modalities, one can effectively leverage the fundamental cognitive framework of the human mind to modify and manipulate the manner in which one represents and processes their concepts and mental constructs. This implies that when utilizing sub-modalities, you are altering the methodology of your thinking. Altering the mode of one's thoughts yields the capacity to modify one's emotions and perspectives pertaining to individuals, relationships, objects, circumstances, surroundings, and contexts. The methods elucidated in this chapter have been carefully orchestrated to assist you in comprehensively grasping the intricacies of a subject matter, individual, circumstance, or environment, with the ultimate objective of enabling a judicious assessment.

Some fundamental methods of NLP that can conveniently be employed are:

Mapping across

Contrastive analysis

Perceptual positions

Swish technique

Mapping across

The term "mapping across" is synonymous with the pattern commonly referred to as the "transition from preference to aversion." This implies the transformation and conversion of one internal representation into another internal representation. For the purpose of illustration, let us consider a scenario where one possesses a preference for and finds pleasure in consuming ice cream, while concurrently harboring distaste and aversion towards frozen yogurt. If one were to employ the method of mapping across, wherein the internal representation of ice cream is altered to that of frozen yogurt, there is a likelihood that a distaste for ice cream would ensue.

Contrastive Analysis

Contrastive analysis entails the examination of the sub-modalities pertaining to two distinct entities. Subsequently, you would engage in a comparative analysis of the two distinct entities to identify their shared characteristics (their mutually shared internal representations). For instance, consider the following scenario: you harbor a distaste for frozen yogurt, yet maintain a fondness for ice cream. Subsequently, undertake a comparative analysis of the ice cream and frozen yogurt, aiming to identify shared characteristics between the two. The internal representation may encompass the aspect that they are both chilled delicacies as well as being derived from milk.

Perceptual Positions

Perceptual positions entail the adoption of three empowered viewpoints when observing an object, individual, circumstance, or contextual setting.

Firstly, it is essential to observe the thing, person, situation, or context from one's own perspective.

Adopt a second perspective - consider the object, individual, circumstance, or context from the viewpoint of another individual.

this person refers to one that is significant to the thing, person, situation or context

Adopting a third-party perspective, analyze the thing, individual, circumstance, or context.

This individual pertains to one who is detached from the object, individual, circumstance, or context.

Swish Technique

The swish technique serves as a method for substituting an unwanted internal representation with a preferred internal representation. For instance, consider the scenario where one possesses the unfavorable tendency to engage in nail-biting behavior during moments of anxiety. An effective approach to address this issue is to transform the reflexive response of nervousness, exemplified by nail-biting, by substituting it with a preferred alternative gesture such as delicately brushing one's hair using fingertips.

The Tripartite Nature of the Mind

The composition of our cognitive faculties encompasses three distinct components: the conscious mind, the subconscious mind, and the unconscious mind. The conscious mind refers to the immediate state of awareness, encompassing one's perception of reality along with the associated knowledge. This information is conveniently accessible for utilization by the intellect. The subconscious mind retains information that is accessible and recoverable, albeit with some degree of effort. The human brain perpetually engages in the processing of subconscious knowledge, albeit without conscious awareness of this ongoing activity.

This definition will be most effectively elucidated through the utilization of an example. Upon entering a familiar setting, we instinctively engage with our surroundings without consciously acknowledging their presence, proceeding in a manner consistent with our past experiences. Likewise, when employing our mother tongue, words flow effortlessly, devoid of any conscious exertion to summon specific vocabulary.

Ultimately, it is the unconscious mind that governs our instincts and the emotions associated with our digestive system. This knowledge, residing in the realms of the unconscious mind, is not presented with the same level of accessibility as the information stored in the conscious or subconscious mind. Although it remains enigmatic to us, it exerts an impact on our actions and precipitates impulsive decision-making.

NLP facilitates the retrieval and acquisition of information housed within the unconscious mind by accumulating knowledge derived from prior experiences, establishing a reservoir of data, and progressively transferring the content from the unconscious to the conscious realm.

Popular Neuro-Linguistics Programming

High-Stress Jobs

Occupations such as medical jurisprudence, security management, and others necessitate a notably elevated level of vigor and exertion. In the event of an accident, individuals are required to consistently communicate with one another throughout the day and remain vigilant. Consequently, in moments of rest, it is imperative for individuals employed in these industries to maintain optimal mental composure, as any lapse in focus can yield momentous and disastrous outcomes. Maintaining focus becomes more challenging when the mind remains in a state of excessive mental exertion and stress.

In such scenarios, even during periods of rest, individuals experience a persistent sense of expectation within their subconscious, ultimately resulting in psychological exhaustion for those operating under such conditions. NLP serves to mitigate such unfavorable situations by promoting individuals to prioritize their mental well-being. It facilitates the management of their repetitive tasks, thereby enhancing their ability to synchronize their personal and professional endeavors effectively.

Planning Jobs

Occupations encompassing fields like business, marketing, and engineering, characterized by the need for significant preparatory efforts, can yield considerable advantages by leveraging the expertise of individuals equipped with NLP training. The possession of a clearly defined objective and the diligent pursuit of it demonstrate a fundamental necessity in the field of NLP, and thereby underscore its significance for individuals engaged in these domains, given that it also serves as a crucial criterion for employment within those professions. The successful execution of long-term projects necessitates the exercise of prudent judgment, a skillset that can be cultivated through the practice of Neuro-Linguistic Programming (NLP).

Creative Works

The pivotal foundation of NLP revolves around challenging preconceived notions, thereby fostering a heightened receptivity of the mind. This particular attribute proves to be advantageous when an individual is engaged in a profession necessitating artistic aptitude, such as that of a visual artist, a literary author, or a thespian. When the principles of NLP are applied, the cognitive faculties are enhanced, enabling the individual to embrace calculated risks and transform them into abundant opportunities. In the realm of thought exploration, the emergence of novel concepts transpires organically once all three cognitive strata have been thoroughly engaged. Additionally, the comprehension of these concepts does not require substantial exertion, as is evident with inexperienced individuals.

Social life

Given the significant importance of personal and professional endeavors, it is equally imperative to consider the social life of individuals in the contemporaneous society. The introduction of novel individuals is presenting chances for fresh encounters, and the exploration of unexplored domains is concurrently enhancing our self-confidence. Various individuals occupy distinct social spheres, ranging from expansive to relatively modest. However, adeptly maintaining a diverse social network signifies an individual's skill in doing so. It is crucial to adeptly manage and navigate one's social connections, striking a harmonious balance that avoids encroaching upon one's personal or occupational endeavors.

An erratic and disorderly social life can be considered a curse disguised as goodwill. Natural Language Processing (NLP) enhances our communicative abilities, as it is imperative to articulate our perspectives without undermining the viewpoints of others. One must find a delicate equilibrium between trust and humility. The practice of NLP cultivates the capacity of our minds to perceive and sustain this state of equilibrium. Stereotyping and generalizing frequently emerge as primary obstacles that necessitate attention when seeking to establish a harmonious social existence. NLP fosters an attitude of receptiveness that contributes to the establishment of a durable community over time.

Relationship

In contemporary times, the management of interpersonal engagements is increasingly challenging owing to the monotonous strain on the human psyche, coupled with the impetuosity and inclination of a majority of individuals to relinquish their efforts prematurely. This leads to catastrophic cases of alienation, divorce, family breakup, etc. Frequently, communication within a familial context tends to become ineffective, as it tends to exacerbate misunderstandings and create divisions. NLP enhances our lives by instilling the essential discipline required to prevent such conflicts, by encouraging the involvement of the subconscious mind while suppressing the inclination to respond aggressively. This objective can be accomplished through the utilization of NLP, which serves to expedite the functioning of the subconscious mind. It cultivates cognitive abilities that empower individuals to express their opinions on significant issues, comprehend differing viewpoints, and foster a mindset that recognizes the triviality of using the game as a means of exploitation. Where there is a difference of opinion between the two parties, a middle ground can be found through mutual consensus or, at the very least, mutual respect can be established. Hence, the formation of mountains from tiny molehills is precluded, hence preventing the escalation of feelings of alienation. Due to the process of globalization, numerous couples reside in different countries in order to pursue their professional endeavors at certain points in their lives. As a result, the issue of infidelity has become widespread due to the rapid pace of travel and the abandonment of prior relationships. The discipline of natural language processing instructs individuals to resist the temptation of a financially advantageous proposition, whether it appeals to their emotional or physical desires. It elevates our moral awareness, ensuring that we refrain from engaging in infidelity within our relationships.

Convictions, Principles, Dispositions, and Conduct

Expanding on the concept of our neural connections and cognitive associations, we further delve into the subject of the outcomes derived from these connections. Our cognitive faculties have the capacity to conceive ideas, which may be selectively retained or rejected based on individual characteristics and underlying motivators.

There exist two types of motivation: intrinsic and extrinsic. Inherent motivation pertains to engaging in an activity, undertaking a pastime, pursuing an exercise, indulging in a hobby, immersing oneself in a field of study, or embarking on a career purely driven by personal interest and the fulfillment it brings. Extrinsic motivation encompasses actions undertaken with the intention of obtaining a reward or, conversely, evading punishment or adverse outcomes.

Through different forms of motivation and the neural connections and associations we develop over the course of our experiences, we shape our system of beliefs, values, attitudes, and behaviors. All these entities coalesce and intertwine, akin to the unified structure of a tree or the intricate network of a neuron within your cognitive faculties. The roots serve as a vital source of nourishment for the trunk, which in turn sustains the branches, ultimately nurturing the growth of the leaves.

Envision, if you will, your system of belief as analogous to a majestic tree. Commencing from the foundational core, we initiate our discourse with convictions.

A belief is a conceptualization that an individual adheres to as a verity. When we designate something as truth, it is typically done based on factors such as certainty, probability, or even the presence of mathematical evidence. These origins can be traced back to various sources, such as cultural and societal conventions, including the religious traditions observed within your community or family. Beliefs find their foundation in personal encounters and explorations of life in general. Additionally, they can be influenced by the opinions and teachings of others, such as mentors, educators, or the broader educational institution. The acquisition of beliefs entails a thorough exploration of all conceivable sources, wherein each one is typically subjected to scrutiny and evaluation until they align with the principles established by one's internal system of beliefs. Once this conviction becomes your reality, it is probable that you will uphold and safeguard it.

Subsequently, we shall delve into the core essence of the tree, namely your values. This is the matter of significance to you. They are derived from conviction, as your convictions serve as a guiding force in determining your core values. A value represents a set of personal principles that serve as a guiding framework for structuring one's life and informing decision-making processes. To attain lucidity, accountability, and coherence in decision-making, individuals must possess knowledge and comprehension of their core values. The ability to express what matters to you is instrumental in making decisions in life.

The branches radiate from the trunk, signifying your perspectives and beliefs. Attitudes depict one's cognitive outlook towards others and the current situation they find themselves in. Your demeanor significantly influences the choices and subsequent conduct that ensue. Attitudes, as perhaps you have surmised, originate from the fundamental framework of your values and beliefs. If one lacks the capacity or inclination to wholeheartedly embrace any set of principles or ideals to navigate their life, their dispositions will be adversely affected, manifesting in attitudes and behaviors such as overly seeking approval, engaging in peer pressure or bullying, harboring worrisome thoughts and anxiety, displaying an excessive preoccupation with others' opinions and judgments about oneself, prioritizing convenience over principles, adhering to political correctness, and so forth.

The foliage of our tree embodies our conduct, particularly in our interactions with others.

The manner in which we conduct ourselves serves as an outward manifestation of our inner experiences or cognitive processes. Our actions are a direct consequence of our origins, core, and extensions. Should your foundation be rooted in an absence of belief, a sole emphasis on personal gain, and a demeanor of moral superiority, it may result in the manifestation of confrontational and potentially detrimental conduct towards both yourself and others. If your foundations are firmly rooted in the principles of prioritizing a quality education, highly valuing achievement in one's profession while maintaining an attitude of respect and professionalism, it is probable that your actions will contribute positively towards achieving your personal aspirations, while also being receptive to the aspirations of others who share a similar journey.

A deficiency in consciousness or recognition of one's values or convictions can impede the adoption of a logical mindset, thereby predisposing individuals to unfavorable or adverse actions. Understanding your personal convictions and values is crucial in shaping your life perspective, which in turn influences your choices and conduct.

Moreover, it is imperative to consider the aspect of motivation. Your tree has flourished by drawing nourishment from either your inherent or external sources of motivation. Do you hold beliefs or place significance in something based on its intriguing and rewarding qualities? Do you place faith in or prioritize something due to apprehension that failing to do so may result in retribution? It is advisable to introspect on one's motivation when undertaking the process of realizing one's truths and values.

Your life's foundation is upheld by your tree of life, and having a clear understanding of your beliefs and priorities is integral to the development of self-awareness. This will provide you with enhanced perception on how to effectively apply NLP techniques to enhance your overall well-being.

Out Frame Reality

This concept is highly sophisticated and deserving of thoughtful consideration. The majority of individuals possess notably frail physiques. One technique used in assertiveness training is referred to as the Broken Record strategy. It implies incessantly reiterating one's perspective until the interlocutor eventually surrenders. For instance, in the event that an individual intends to obtain a reimbursement and possesses a valid proof of purchase, it is advised to consistently reiterate the following statement:

Certainly, I comprehend your concern and I request a reimbursement."

Irrespective of the individual's articulated responses, whether it be claiming a heavy workload or lacking the necessary expertise, persistently reiterate the aforementioned concise assertion until they ultimately relinquish their stance. The hypothesis posits that individuals possess a limited quantity of negative responses within their capacity. Once their supply is depleted, they will adhere to your instructions without hesitation. By engaging in the daily practice of reframing, and gradually recognizing your capacity to attribute significance to events, you will gradually incorporate this process into your real-time experiences.

Humorous Yet Practical Illustration

Imagine that you assume the role of a sales representative. And through repeated practice, you have become proficient enough in this exercise to interpret any customer behavior as a genuine indication of their intention to make a purchase. Suppose one holds a firm belief in a given matter, exhibiting neither forceful nor coercive sales tactics. Let us envision you as a character partaking in a comedic narrative. Irrespective of the customer's statements, you diligently perceive those as valid justifications for their desire to acquire the product. If they state that they are solely browsing, you may respond in the following manner: "

Given our mutual understanding, it is evident that your appreciation for this product is genuine, and your intention is to challenge me to earn my commission. I sincerely value your support. May I kindly inquire about your preferred payment method?

If you were to express the aforementioned sentiment with utmost sincerity and a pleasantly radiant countenance, it is likely that the customer would be prompted to burst into amusement. If one were to employ such an approach consistently, ingeniously manipulating the articulated ideas, it is plausible that it could result in a potential purchase of the product. However, this necessitates a genuine alignment on your end. If, in fact, they were to depart, you would still maintain the belief that it would serve as a clear demonstration of their genuine interest in purchasing the product. Whilst this illustration may appear implausible and exaggerated, it serves to underscore the notion that if one were to genuinely subscribe to the notion that every uttered statement signifies an intention to make a purchase, they would inadvertently internalize this perspective as well. The majority of individuals possess limited autonomy in determining their perception of reality. Numerous studies have demonstrated that individuals possessing a robust frame, whereby frame refers to their interpretation or perspective of events, are likely to influence and persuade others more effectively. Engaging in this exercise will bestow upon you a plethora of physical prowess and adaptability in the manner you attribute significance to occurrences. The majority of individuals do not entertain the notion that events possess any significance beyond the immediate interpretations that come to mind. As you engage in this exercise with increasing duration and authenticity, you will gradually realize that a significant portion of what we commonly perceive as "reality" falls within the realm of your control.

Why is NLP Good For You?

Natural Language Processing (NLP) possesses the ability to facilitate the emergence of novel prospects and catalyze transformative alterations in people's lives. It has the potential to foster emotions, promote constructive conduct, and facilitate the resolution of internal struggles.

Gaining a comprehensive comprehension of NLP's efficacy can facilitate advancements across various domains of your life. This includes enhancing interpersonal connections, mastering instructional techniques, bolstering self-assurance and drive, refining communication and comprehension skills, optimizing professional prospects, and optimizing cognitive processes, thoughts, and behaviors.

Which individuals can derive advantages from natural language processing (NLP)?

The short answer is: ANYONE, anyone on the planet going through life and facing its ups and downs. We may not always have jurisdiction over the unfolding of events in our lives, but we do have agency in determining our responses. Recognizing this truth bestows upon us an entirely fresh outlook on life. NLP can be of utmost assistance in this regard.

If you engage in interpersonal interactions.

Seeking to enhance interpersonal connections.

Have a keen interest in self-development.

Do you find yourself hindered by the impacts of your past on your endeavors?

Desire to enhance one's proficiency in a particular area.

You have the potential to greatly enhance the quality of your life.

In that case, you will be able to derive advantages from the implementation of NLP techniques.

Applications of NLP

Personal Development

Assume control over your own existence. Utilize natural language processing (NLP) to eliminate adverse emotions, principles, and counterproductive decision-making methodologies. You will eradicate undesirable behaviors from your lifestyle, such as smoking, excessive eating, excessive fixation, unhealthy relationships, and other behaviors that are fostering toxicity in your life. You will assume command over your cognitive functions and assert authority over the course of your life, rather than allowing external factors to dictate your destiny.

If you are encountering obstacles in your present life due to unresolved issues from the past, NLP offers a means by which you can manipulate and recalibrate your subconscious mind to diminish the significance of these prior memories. With the application of NLP, one can effortlessly activate the motivational mechanism within the mind and sustain determination in the pursuit of one's objectives. In addition, you can enhance your aptitude for learning by acquainting yourself with the distinctive cognitive techniques that align with your individual brain.

Counseling

Natural Language Processing (NLP) is widely regarded as the preeminent approach for effecting expeditious and enduring transformations. Neuro-Linguistic Programming offers an expeditious means to eradicate addictive behaviors, alleviate anxiety and depression, reconcile distorted self-perceptions, discard undesirable conduct, and recondition unfavorable beliefs.

Sales And Marketing

Through the application of NLP, you will acquire the necessary abilities to establish instant and significant rapport with your clients. You will gain the ability to interpret their nonverbal cues, discern the sincerity of their words, and adapt your communicative abilities to align with their preferred style. This can result in an increase in revenue.

Business

By gaining a thorough understanding of the decision-making strategies and principles of your business associates, customers, and employees, you have the opportunity to cultivate a commanding sense of stability within your organization. This will enable you to effectively strategize, proficiently allocate tasks, determine suitable candidates for employment and positions, and invigorate the business. By leveraging the principles of NLP, you will acquire the skills necessary to effectively navigate negotiations and adeptly address challenges, thereby enhancing the likelihood of attaining success in your business endeavors.

Family Relations

Proactively prevent conflicts. Enhance interpersonal communication within your familial relations. Strive to enhance your abilities as a companion, caregiver, sibling, offspring, or progeny. Enhance the quality of your marital relationship and rekindle the fervor that once characterized it. Instill in your children the values and skills necessary to actively engage in and positively impact society.

Education

Utilize natural language processing techniques to adapt instructional strategies to the distinctive cognitive aspects of your mind. Maximize your personal capacity for learning. Students often achieve lackluster outcomes due to their cognitive processing differing from the conventional methods employed. Modify your communication style to yield favorable and constructive results. NLP offers a potential solution for addressing learning deficiencies, Attention Deficit Disorder, and hyperactivity. The anxiety associated with test-taking, performance anxiety, and aversion to specific academic subjects can be effectively mitigated by employing Neuro-Linguistic Programming (NLP) techniques.

Sports

The exceptional performance in sports is primarily ascribed to the mindset of the athlete. If an athlete is not in an optimal condition, then he will be unable to perform at his maximum potential. Altering one's mindset can facilitate athletes in achieving levels of success previously unanticipated. NLP is employed in a dynamic manner to facilitate Olympic athletes in achieving the pinnacle of innovative performance.

Utilizing Neuro-Linguistic Programming to Transform our Lifestyle

Once we acquire an understanding of our personal perception of reality, we gain the ability to enact modifications in order to achieve the desired life experiences. It is possible for us to gain insights into the responses of others towards the specific situation that we are currently encountering. We acknowledge the disparities pertaining to the approaches employed and the outcomes obtained. We relinquish our personal compass and immerse ourselves in unfamiliar territories. As soon as this occurrence takes place, anticipatory benefits shall be forthcoming to you. Your life shall undergo a noteworthy transformation that will forever alter its course.

Natural Language Processing (NLP) enhances the intricacy and effectiveness of our interpersonal connections, commencing with our self-awareness and extending to personal and close associations. Furthermore, it extends its influence to our occupational and professional endeavors, and ultimately permeates the realm of restorative practices involving collaborative efforts aimed at fostering healing, advancement, and transformation. NLP provides us with the means to enhance our own well-being as well as that of others.

Restructuring: Ingenuity or evasion of reality?

On certain occasions, it proves immensely beneficial to adopt alternate viewpoints when considering situations, events, or objects. It is particularly advantageous when you have recently arrived at the juncture of stagnation. Psychology provides the technique of reframing as an approach to achieve this objective, a technique that is also employed within the framework of neuro-linguistic programming. Since NLP employs the mechanism of reinterpretation to gain fresh perspectives and thereby make progress towards the resolution. Reframing proves beneficial not only during moments of crisis, but also in daily existence, fostering a more optimistic outlook and heightened contentment. What exactly is meant by reframing and what are its mechanisms?

Reconceptualizing - Reexamining through systematic approach: a single delineation

Frame pertains to a protocol utilized in the context of neurolinguistic programming and family therapy. The act of reframing is a commonplace occurrence that transpires on a daily basis for individuals, frequently transpiring without their conscious awareness. Consequently, occurrences are understood and analyzed within the context of specific anticipations, cognitive patterns, and designated roles. They consequently provide them with a specific structure, which, based on the prevailing perspective, manifests itself in varying ways. This leads to either a favorable or unfavorable reinterpretation.

Over time, it proves to be a formidable challenge to coexist with negative interpretations due to their inherent imposition of unacceptable limitations on selective aspects. All individuals desiring to effect change often employ the practice of positive thinking as a means to take actionable steps towards their objectives. From a theoretical standpoint, what we are essentially discussing here is a process akin to reframing or neuro-linguistic programming, wherein our perspective shifts from perceiving things in a negative light to viewing them through a positive lens. However, could you please elucidate the workings of Reframing? It is very easy. You assign a novel and distinct connotation to an occurrence or a specific circumstance through its association with an alternative framework. To demonstrate this point, let me provide a few instances.

One's perception of a situation is contingent upon several factors. These factors encompass the diurnal pattern and fundamental demeanor, wherein it may oscillate between a positive inclination or a relatively negative predisposition. This phenomenon is manifested in the act of redefining the perspective for both situations. Consider a glass of water that is halfway filled. You may be familiar with the renowned inquiry: "Does the glass possess half its capacity or is it lacking half its capacity?" When considering this matter impartially, the outcome consistently remains unchanged. Nevertheless, numerous aspects are contingent upon one's point of view. The subsequent examples provided derive from practical experiences in the professional realm:

- In the event that your supervisor is vocally demonstrating displeasure towards you immediately upon your arrival at the workplace in the early hours of the day, it is plausible that they may have experienced a negative start to their day or engaged in a conflict with their spouse or children during the early morning hours.

- There is a silver lining to the situation of not securing the desired occupation, as it allows you to remain in your comforting, affectionate surroundings without the necessity of relocating.

These instances unavoidably prompt the inquiry as to whether the act of reframing is potentially a repudiation of facts or a resourceful approach to managing situation. Skeptics deem it a form of self-delusion, given that this method is employed to render unfavorable circumstances more palatable. Nevertheless, individuals who merely expound upon the positive aspects in an elegant fashion exhibit a lack of comprehension regarding the principles of reframing and neuro-linguistic programming. Ultimately, it does not revolve around suppressing disagreeable aspects and emotions and promptly adopting an optimistic outlook, thereby establishing a comforting atmosphere. Similar to positive sensations and thought patterns, negative and unpleasant circumstances, thoughts, and emotions, such as anger or grief, are entitled to their existence.

Reframing involves identifying the optimal balance or equilibrium. As an illustration, Intveen asserts:

It is commonly acknowledged that the reception of negative information has a profound impact on one's cognitive processes, making it challenging to maintain clarity of thought. In common parlance, this is referred to as a strike to the frontal region. The cerebral cortex is currently being subjected to a surge of stress hormones. They give rise to an abrupt impediment to cognitive processes.

A considerable number of individuals have a tendency to excessively focus on this deficit. Only the conspicuous is observed, namely the entities that promptly become prominent. The splendid occurrences and modest triumphs that once graced our existence have regrettably receded into the realm of obscurity.

Revisiting the occurrence of the dream job being rescinded, it must be noted that indulging in self-deception would entail convincing oneself of having no desire for the position whatsoever. By doing so, you effectively set aside your negative emotions. In the interim, you hinder your ability to engage in introspection. Presumably, there were discernible factors that prevented you from acquiring this coveted position.

When reframing is employed, the experienced situation acquires entirely novel dimensions. In order to achieve success, one must pose the fundamental question: "For what purpose?" Frequently, the initial inquiry posed is: "For what reason have I been chosen?"

Intveen provides a cogent insight into the lack of utility associated with posing inquiries pertaining to the rationale behind something. She presumes that the attention is fixated on the issue. An individual's cognitive processes often exhibit a cyclical pattern, in which thoughts continually circulate without the ability to cease or disengage from this loop. There are no sufficient answers that meet the desired level of satisfaction. It is possible that you could obtain them by making an inquiry with the company. However, one cannot ascertain with certainty that a truthful response will be obtained.

Conversely, when the question is initiated with "what for", it prompts an exploration of the context and the potential for a fresh framework.

What is the purpose behind receiving a rejection?

What are the benefits of remaining employed within the company and maintaining a sense of familiarity within the environment?

● For what purposes can the acquired experience be utilized?

NLP Techniques

Allow us to explore a set of methodologies that can facilitate our connection with our perceptual and cognitive processes. It is an established fact that the world can be an intimidating environment, and it is unrealistic to expect that we can exert complete control over every aspect of it. However, it is within our capacity to exercise self-control and regulate our responses to external stimuli by diligently training our mental faculties.

Method 1: Rediscovering a Positive Outlook
Individuals with distinct cognitive processes will exhibit varied responses to life events, thereby highlighting pronounced dissimilarities rooted in their unique emotional perspectives.

Should an individual experience a consistent state of joy, it is due to their ability to cultivate the habit of perceiving the positive aspects of life. Indeed, while they may encounter moments of financial strain, their attention will not be fixated on such periods, as they understand that they are transient in nature.

An individual experiencing depression tends to fixate on the negative aspects of their life, rendering them incapable of perceiving the world as it truly exists. One fundamental disparity between these two individuals lies in their respective perspectives on the world.

In the course of one's lifetime, there will be periods characterized by favorable circumstances, as well as occasions where it may seem that adversity prevails. An individual who exudes a higher degree of optimism regarding life is inclined to view any setbacks encountered as ephemeral in nature, with the assured belief that they will eventually subside. This enhances an individual's resilience, enabling them to recover more swiftly from adverse circumstances compared to individuals experiencing depression.

An individual who experiences depression tends to perceive their setbacks as perpetually enduring. Every negative experience appears interminable, regardless of its duration, to individuals suffering from depression. They may perceive a mere day as stretching into a month, and a week as extending into a year. It will create the perception that their experience is enduring indefinitely, with no prospects for improvement in the foreseeable future.

They will not recover as swiftly from adversities in their life compared to individuals who actively seek out the positives.

When experiencing depression, one acquires a persistent sense of pessimism that permeates their emotions. It is not an inherent trait. This condition is commonly referred to as chronic pervasive negativity or acquired powerlessness. Nevertheless, it is possible to circumvent this learned helplessness.

The primary distinction between an optimist and a pessimist lies in the fact that an optimist possesses the skill to articulate their rationale when faced with adversity. They possess the capacity to engage in discussion regarding the subject matter, which in turn grants them the ability to seek out the positive aspects amidst their surroundings.

An individual who possesses a consistently pessimistic outlook on life will face difficulties in discussing their personal challenges, consequently leading to their continuous stagnation in the unfavorable situation they currently find themselves in.

The initial course of action to cease this acquired state of helplessness involves acknowledging the recurring patterns that will precipitate your immersion into this predicament. Once you start to perceive that you consistently focus on the negative aspects of existence, you will inadvertently be directing yourself towards a path characterized by learned helplessness. However, with the aid of NLP, it is possible to overcome this obstacle.

Several instances of this can be observed, such as keeping in mind that the negative occurrences are transient in nature and confined solely to the particular circumstances you are currently facing. Adverse occurrences such as experiencing a phase in your employment where your working hours are diminished, will only be transitory in nature. Should the need arise, it is possible for you to secure alternative employment in order to ensure sufficient hours and maintain your accustomed level of income.

Inevitably, you will encounter trials and tribulations throughout the course of your life. Nevertheless, your approach to handling the situation will depend on your cognitive process in relation to that particular challenge. One's perspective has the power to cast a favorable or unfavorable light upon every aspect of their existence.

Presented below is an illustrative instance that effectively demonstrates the implementation of this methodology. When confronted with future challenges, consider them as valuable chances for personal development. Follow these steps:

Firstly, it is important to acknowledge and come to terms with the fact that you are currently faced with a challenge. The majority of individuals have a tendency to downplay the magnitude of the problem or deny its existence in order to avoid acknowledging its occurrence. However, to surmount the obstacle, it is imperative to acknowledge the presence of the challenge and commit to conquering it. Please document a concise overview of the issue currently being discussed.

Step two: Take action. No obstacle can be effectively overcome through complacency and inaction. Thus, devise a strategic framework that will enable you to effectively surmount this obstacle, in order to subsequently implement it. Compose a roster comprising a minimum of three sequential tasks aimed at achieving a more optimistic outcome.

Proceed to the third step: Assess all available information pertaining to the given situation. What sources are available for you to overcome this obstacle? Determining the most effective resources to assist you will serve as an invaluable means of discerning the necessary steps to overcome this challenge. For instance, in the event that you encounter difficulty comprehending a particular concept, it would be advisable to approach a colleague and inquire if they possess an alternative way of articulating it, thereby enabling your comprehension. Engage in conversations with individuals who possess the necessary knowledge and expertise to provide you with insights into the complexities of your life. If you encounter challenges in your professional or academic environment, it is advisable to engage in a constructive conversation with your supervisor or instructor in order to resolve the issues at hand. You might discover that seeking guidance from your acquaintances and loved ones can provide valuable insights.

Fourth step: Uncertain of any further courses of action? Conduct thorough research. The internet provides a plethora of accounts from individuals who have encountered analogous experiences to yours, and they possess the requisite knowledge that will assist you in overcoming this predicament. Furthermore, it should be noted that you will have the opportunity to locate books that can provide valuable assistance should you choose to pursue that path. This serves as an effective means to alleviate the sense of isolation that accompanies the experience, by providing reassurance that you are not alone in navigating these circumstances.

Step five: Examine the range of potential alternatives presented by each option available to you. Every decision carries distinct consequences, and it is imperative to ascertain the potential outcomes associated with each choice made. Please ascertain and document several of the alternatives available to you.

Step six: On occasion, it may be necessary to seek the guidance and tutelage of a mentor in order to successfully navigate and overcome the challenges you encounter. Seek the counsel or guidance of an individual with whom you can engage in meaningful conversation. This does not necessarily require the presence of a physical individual; it can also encompass a digital platform or a literary publication. However, it is essential to exercise caution when engaging in conversations, ensuring that the individual with whom you are interacting can be relied upon to maintain your confidentiality and genuinely provide assistance, rather than offering unhelpful or insincere remarks.

Proceed to the seventh step: Monitor the progress of your undertaking. Maintain a comprehensive documentation of your progress as you execute the action steps towards achieving a more favorable outcome.

Assumption 9: Individuals exhibit flawless efficacy in generating the outcomes they currently attain.

The meaning:

You consistently demonstrate exceptional work performance, and although you may have made mistakes in the past, your work has always been exemplary. I understand that you have committed numerous errors in the past and subsequently experienced regret. And I know if you just could have an opportunity to back to the past to change again your life.

I understand your desire for a different outcome, however, it is important to note that during the occurrence in question, your actions were not erroneous. And what I am implying is that your course of action was based on your best judgement.

Perhaps the course of action you believed to be appropriate at that moment might have been incorrect; one can never be certain.

The mentality you possessed during that period is not reflective of the mentality you currently possess. Hence, you believe that your previous performance was not impeccable.

It is important for you to understand that your work was impeccable at that time; however, you have currently decided to alter your viewpoint on it.

The course of action you are advised to pursue:

Cease dwelling on the actions of the past and harboring feelings of remorse. I understand that you may be inclined to view yourself as unintelligent during that period, but in reality, you were not. You simply made the most suitable decision based on the resources and mindset available to you at that time.

Remain mindful of the current circumstance, seize the instant, and engage in proactive conduct. If one's current circumstances are a result of a misguided past decision, it is imperative to effectuate change by focusing on those aspects that are within one's control, rather than lamenting over the past. Naturally, it is imperative that one learns from their past missteps;

however, the sole course of action available is to effect a modification in the present.

"The advantages you will receive:

You will become an individual who achieves superior outcomes and attains notable accomplishments. Consider the implications of consistently reflecting upon past errors, strategically determining a path of progress, and effecting transformative actions. However, by directing your attention towards present modifications and implementing decisive measures, you will progress and ultimately attain the status of a triumphant individual.

Another benefit is the capacity to release it. And that entails relinquishing the past, relinquishing the negative recollections, relinquishing previous errors... Consequently, this grants one the ability to live with sound mental wellness. Regarding mental well-being, adopting a mindful approach entails redirecting one's thoughts away from the past, thereby granting the opportunity to cultivate mindfulness and embrace the present moment.

Assertion 10: Failure is Nonexistent; Feedback Prevails

"I have not failed. I have recently discovered 10,000 approaches that are ineffective." - Thomas Edison

The meaning:

It is highly likely that you frequently encounter instances of failure in your life. Notably, similar to the majority of individuals, one tends to abhor the experience of failure, perceiving it as a potential obstacle in attaining desired objectives. However, if I were to inform you that you have never experienced failure, but rather have approached tasks in an ineffective manner.

Many individuals, upon experiencing failure, hastily surrender. They hold the belief that they have experienced a failure, but this assertion lacks veracity. Their failure can be attributed to their insufficient attempts, as well as their tendency to persist with unvarying approaches.

If one experiences a setback in any pursuit, it does not equate to failure per se; rather, it signifies that a mistake has been made. By adopting the correct approach, one can attain success.

In my perspective, failure is not merely the absence of success in one's endeavors, but rather, it manifests when one chooses to surrender and forfeit their efforts.

"The recommended course of action:

If one desires to attain a specific objective and repeatedly encounters failure, it is advisable to desist from engaging in identical actions, as persevering in such a manner will only yield identical outcomes. Instead, endeavor to experience novel activities until you discover the optimal course of action to attain your objective.

Consider the contrasting methods employed by a mouse and a fly when attempting to make their exit from an enclosed space. The fly consistently seeks to free itself from the confines of the window pane, persistently repeating its attempts to escape. Unfortunately, its endeavors prove futile, resulting in its inability to successfully break free. Of course, given its vulnerable position on the glass surface, it becomes a simple task to eliminate the fly. Now consider the behavior of a mouse upon its escape; it consistently attempts to find alternate routes throughout the room, rendering it challenging for us to apprehend the mouse when it is present within an enclosed space. Adopt the perspective of a mouse rather than that of a fly.

When experiencing a setback (i.e., encountering a situation in which your efforts prove futile), it is imperative to extract valuable insights from such experiences. Reflect on the reasons for your failure, pinpoint the error you committed, consider strategies for improvement, and devise preventive measures to avoid a recurrence of said mistake.

Understand that failure serves as a stepping stone towards achieving success and as a necessary cost for attaining it. Make persistent attempts and persevere without surrendering.

The advantages you will receive:

Consider the impact of consistently experiencing setbacks over a prolonged period of time. How might one's resilience and outlook be affected after numerous attempts and ongoing struggle? You will develop into an individual with a wealth of experience, equipping you with the ability to excel in various domains of your life. Furthermore, cultivating a plethora of life experiences contributes to the development of emotional and mental resilience, fortifying one's character. And the most exemplary aspect of everything I have stated is that eventually, you shall emerge triumphant and realize the fulfillment of the dream you have tirelessly striven for. Triumph is most gratifying when it is the fruit of diligent effort.

Practical task

Are there any challenges that you believe are not adequately supported due to insufficient resources available?

For instance, you are required to perform tasks that do not elicit a sense of enthusiasm. You are unable to gather strength and continue towards it.

Consider the potential avenues for obtaining the necessary resources to complete the task at hand.

There exist, at a minimum, two different approaches to this situation.

Firstly, one can visualize the outcome of their efforts, perceiving it as already accomplished and satisfying. Envision the completion of the task at hand. Take pleasure in the sensation of contentment and happiness for your own self. If the outcome is discernible, commend it internally. This will assist you in restoring the internal reserves necessary to perform the task.

Additionally, you have the option of reflecting upon a task that you carried out with great zeal, wherein you were fully invested as a valuable asset. Engage in a cognitive shift to adopt this particular mindset. This will assist in the restoration of your working condition and facilitate the completion of the task with greater ease.

Please bear in mind that you possess an abundant reserve of resources that is not easily depleted. Establish an objective to locate them in any circumstance where their demand arises. By doing so, you will assuredly uncover not merely one, but numerous reservoirs of resources that can profoundly enhance your existence.

Practical task

Determining the preeminent representative system that pertains to you is an effortless task.

Envision yourself amidst a wooded area, or along a coastal shore, or within a blossoming landscape, and endeavor to discern the primary sensory impression that emerged within you: whether it was visual, auditory, or kinesthetic. To clarify, did you visually perceive the imagery, audibly perceive sounds such as the crashing of waves or the chirping of birds, or sensory experience the aromas, warmth, and gentle breeze?

One might be under the impression that these images materialized concurrently. However, it should be noted that one of the three representative systems was operational slightly prior, subsequently influencing the timing of the remaining two systems. Consider alternative visualizations - for instance, envision the presence of a watermelon before you. Which preceded the other - an image, or the sensations of taste, smell, or perhaps the accompanying sound of its creation?

Additionally, be mindful of the type of images, whether they are visual, auditory, or kinesthetic, that prove simpler for you to retain, as well as those that manifest with greater clarity, vividness, and explicitness in your imagination. Perhaps you possess a keen ability to imagine auditory sensations, while your recollection of the visual elements appears somewhat indistinct? This is characteristic of an individual with a preference for auditory stimuli. Alternatively, if, conversely, you possess a distinct and unambiguous "visual perception" of the scenario, with the sounds fading into oblivion or appearing incomprehensible, it is highly likely that you possess traits consistent with the visual cognitive style. If one were to initially recall their sensations, such as smell, taste, temperature, tension, relaxation, comfort, or discomfort, it can be reasonably inferred that they belong to the kinesthetic category of individuals.

None of these three types are inherently inferior to one another! However, it is only through the collective functioning and harmonious collaboration of all three representative systems that we can attain the entirety of worldly insights and understanding.

There exist alternative methodologies that can enable you to ascertain, with a considerable level of precision, the predominant representative system that aligns with your preferences. Furthermore, it is worth noting that these techniques possess the capacity to enhance one's comprehension not only of oneself, but also of others.

Initially, one can choose to adhere to their own or another individual's discourse. The frequency with which we employ certain words is a highly accurate reflection of our highly representative system.

Additionally, one can acquire knowledge pertaining to representative systems by examining an individual's preferences, inclinations, and the areas of their focused attention.

Additionally, one can observe the direction of an individual's gaze as they engage in cognitive processes and conjure specific mental imagery.

Typically, the movement of our eyes varies based on the nature of the signals we perceive, be it visual, auditory, or kinesthetic.

Allow us to examine these three tricks in greater depth.

The manner in which speech articulates representative systems

If you possess a proclivity for visual stimuli, it is likely that your speech will incorporate an abundance of visual-related vocabulary and expressions.

• It is apparent.

• Brilliant prospects,

• Perspective on the issue

In my perspective, "In my viewpoint, "According to my observation, "Based on my analysis, "In light of my evaluation, "From my vantage point,

• I perceive it from my own perspective,

• Depending on one's perspective, • Depending on the vantage point, • Depending on the viewpoint, • Depending on the angle of observation,

• From my perspective, • In my viewpoint, • Considering the facts, •

Based on my observation, • It is my belief, • I hold the opinion that, • In my estimation, • It is my contention that, • As I see it,

• Apparently,

• It is evident, • It is apparent, • It is obvious, • It is apparent from observed data/evidence, • There is no doubt,

• Do you represent?

If you possess a proclivity towards audio stimuli, it is likely that you frequently incorporate lexicon associated with auditory perception into your discourse, such as:

• Unprecedented business venture • Novel and unfamiliar business • Unexplored and unfamiliar industry • Uncharted territory in business

• I am not interested in discussing it. • I prefer not to entertain the topic. • I would rather not be informed about it. • It is not of relevance to me.

I was informed of your statement.

- It appears to be an enticing prospect.

- This is the first instance in which I have been made aware of.

- It necessitates further deliberation

- It is self-evident, • It is patently clear, • It is apparent, • It is undeniable, • It is self-explanatory, • It is obvious.

- There is no information regarding you. • Your name hasn't been mentioned. • There is a lack of knowledge pertaining to your existence. • Your presence has not been acknowledged.

- Establish a shared means of communication, • Identify a mutually understood form of language, • Determine a universal mode of expression, • Foster a collective understanding of communication.

- It aligns with my current mood.

If you possess a kinesthetic inclination, your speech will exhibit an ample array of terms pertaining to sensations, such as:

• Nice atmosphere,

• Warm welcome,

• Cold look,

• It caused me emotional distress.

• In my opinion, • It is my belief that, • From my perspective, • I am of the opinion that, • It is my view that, • I think that,

• We shall refrain from interfering with this matter.

• According to my personal preference, • Based on my personal opinion, • From my perspective, • In my estimation,

• I was extremely surprised,

• Displeased countenance, • Disgruntled visage, • Unhappy demeanor, • Frowning visage, • Morose facial expression, • Grimace of dissatisfaction, • Glum and discontented face, • Look of sourness.

• Tough measures.

Practical task

Recall a particular episode from your personal experiences, ideally one that holds positive associations and is of significance to you, and that you are keen to discuss. Verbally express it spontaneously, devoid of premeditation or deliberate contemplation, without prior rehearsal of your narrative. This activity can be conducted in collaboration with a partner. Kindly request them to acquire a notebook and a writing instrument, and proceed to record words pertaining to "visual", "auditory", and "kinesthetic" aspects from your discourse.

However, one can easily document their narrative using a recording device and subsequently analyze the frequency of different categories of words and expressions through independent calculation. By doing so, the prominent representative structure will be exposed.

The correlation between representative systems and our predispositions and preferred pastimes

If one possesses a proclivity towards visual stimuli, one may find enjoyment in pursuits pertaining to visual perception, such as:

• Luminous, exquisite, trendy, elegant attire;

• The interiors are exquisitely and elegantly decorated.

• Attendance at cultural institutions, showcases;

- Place importance on their physical presentation;
- Concern themselves with how they look;
- Value their external appearance;

- Courses in the fields of photography, painting, and other forms of visual arts;

- All magnificent artistic mediums - theatre, film, television;

- Guided tours, journeys offering opportunities to explore cultural landmarks, tourist attractions, and the scenic splendor of nature;

- Maintaining cleanliness and organization in both domestic and professional environments.

If you have a preference for auditory experiences, you are inclined towards everything pertaining to the perception of sound.

- Music;

- Telephone conversations;

- Natural sounds;

- Audio recordings transmitted via radio and literature narrated in audio format;

- Beautiful voices;

- Articulating your thoughts audibly even in the absence of an audience;

- Deliberations, exchanging perspectives; • Dialogues, sharing opinions; • Converse, communing thoughts; • Consultations, conveying viewpoints; • Discourse, interchanging ideas.

- Maintaining absolute silence during periods of work and rest.

"If you exhibit a preference for kinesthetic experiences, you derive enjoyment from sensory stimuli that are pleasurable in nature:

- Attire and footwear that offer convenience and comfort;

- Massage;

- The disciplines of gymnastics, various sports, and dancing;

- The house is characterized by a pleasant warmth and a sense of comfort;

- Enjoyable scents, delectable cuisine;

- Thermal therapy facilities like saunas, steam baths, and hydrotherapy treatments;

- The chairs are plush and cozy, while the bed offers a high level of comfort.

- Relaxation, rest, peace.

Practical task

Through an assessment of your proclivities and behaviors, undertake an examination to ascertain the predominant representative system within you. It is highly probable that you will observe indications of all three systems - this occurrence is standard, as all three systems are operational.

While your appreciation for elegant attire is evident, it is crucial that you prioritize your personal comfort. Alternatively, do you have an appreciation for museums and attend performances of high-quality music? Alternatively, are you fond of delectable cuisine while simultaneously prioritizing your aesthetic appearance?

Nevertheless, it is apparent that indicators of a specific framework are predominant within your being. Alternatively, of greater significance to you is the correlation between specific systems. For instance, if you possess an affinity for both aesthetics and comfort in attire, it is probable that you will prioritize convenience and refrain from wearing garments that cause discomfort, despite their attractiveness.

Examine yourself closely, and you will invariably discover that one of the three systems within you is more operationally prevalent.

Neuro-Linguistic Programming in Therapeutic Practice

One can succinctly encapsulate a fundamental concept of Neuro-Linguistic Programming (N.L.P.) with the adage, "The map is not the territory," as it underscores the divergences between subjective belief and objective truth. It highlights the tendency of every individual to operate within their subjective perspective rather than from an objective standpoint. Proponents of N.L.P. acknowledge that each individual's perception of the world is distorted, restricted, and unique in nature. A practitioner of N.L.P. should, hence, gain an understanding of how a person undergoing treatment perceives their cognitive framework, commonly referred to as their "map," and recognize the potential influence this perception can have on their thoughts and actions.

An individual's perception of the world is molded by the acquired knowledge facilitated by their cognitive abilities. This data may encompass information pertaining to sound, visual elements, odors, tastes, or sensory experiences. N.L.P. professionals acknowledge the distinct variations in quality and significance in this data, while emphasizing that each individual procedural experience employed a fundamental illustrative framework known as P.R.S. In order for an N.L.P. advisor to effectively assist an individual undergoing treatment, it is essential for the specialist to strive to align the person's Personal Representation System (P.R.S.) with their guide. N.L.P. experts acknowledge the possibility of accessing genuine systems by employing cues such as eye movements.

N.L.P. professionals collaborate with individuals to grasp their cognitive processes, ethical principles, emotional states, and expectations. By conducting an analysis of an individual's guide, the specialist is able to provide assistance in identifying and enhancing the skills that are most beneficial to them, while also aiding in the development of novel strategies to replace ineffective ones. This procedure has the potential to assist individuals undergoing treatment in reaching their treatment goals.

Advocates of N.L.P. assert that this approach ensures expedited and lasting outcomes, while enhancing one's understanding of subjective experiences and ethical principles. N.L.P. also endeavors to establish effective communication between conscious and unconscious mental processes in order to aid individuals in enhancing their creativity and problem-solving capabilities. Some advocates of N.L.P. differentiate the approach from cognitive behavioral therapy (C.B.T.) but assert that N.L.P. can yield significant improvements in a shorter duration. From its inception, neuro-linguistic programming has been applied to address a wide range of concerns. These include:

Anxiety, apprehension, and agitation

Correspondence issues
Posttraumatic stress
Melancholy
Insufficient attentiveness and hyperactivity Insufficiency in attention and hyperactivity Lack of attention and hyperactivity Attention deficit and hyperactivity
Compulsion
Schizophrenia
Obsessions and urges
Marginal character

RESEARCH ON NEURO-LINGUISTIC PROGRAMMING

Despite being limited in quantity, thorough investigations have explored the efficacy of N.L.P. as a therapeutic approach. In a recent study, experts investigated the potential of implementing neuro-linguistic programming techniques to enhance the educational experience of children with special needs, who require more strategic organization within the classroom setting. Researchers have successfully completed Natural Language Processing (N.L.P.) protocols, which assisted in cultivating a constructive mindset among children, thereby facilitating effective and enhanced learning. It was further elucidated that these outcomes were deemed as "concise and tentative conclusions", despite the presence of other constraining factors, as the sample size encompassed merely seven children.

N.L.P. experts assert that changes in one's eye movements can serve as a reliable indicator for detecting falsehood. In the year of 2012, experts conducted an examination of this case in a series of three consecutive proceedings. In the initial study, the ocular advancements observed in individuals who were being truthful or deceptive did not align with the presumed patterns suggested by N.L.P. In the ensuing inquiry, a particular group was informed about the theory of eye movements in neuro-linguistic programming (N.L.P.). Simultaneously, the benchmark group unequivocally was not. There was negligible disparity between the two groups following the administration of a deception recognition test. During the third inquiry, the ocular advancements of every faction were recorded during public interviews. Furthermore, there existed no discernible disparity in the progression of ocular development amongst them.

In 2012, experts conducted a comprehensive investigation into the impact of N.L.P. on the well-being of individuals. Currently, an assessment was conducted regarding various concerns encompassing substance abuse, anxiety, weight management, morning sickness, and claustrophobia. The analysts deduced that although conclusive evidence was lacking to substantiate the ineffectiveness of N.L.P., there was scant evidence to suggest that

N.L.P. interventions enhanced well-being.

Managing Your Mind

Permit yourself to embrace the implausible

To alter your habits or thought patterns, it is imperative to resist the inclination to adhere to the belief that change is unattainable. This is a common impediment that frequently hinders individuals, namely the conviction that their present state will persist indefinitely. Dismiss this notion, as it will merely impede your personal growth and hinder your journey towards self-actualization.

Grant yourself the authority to achieve success.

A widespread belief ingrained in the subconscious of numerous individuals is that they will never attain the level of success they desire. Certain individuals develop psychological issues due to their upbringing in poverty, leading them to believe that they will never attain sufficient financial resources and should perpetually adopt a mindset of financial scarcity. We persist in our lack of success, both in various other regards. There exists a group of individuals who hold the belief that they lack the capability to engage in creative pursuits or perform specific types of work. One must revise their mindset, and upon recognizing such thoughts stemming from their subconscious, they should consciously affirm their own capabilities and potential for success.

Resist others' projections
Each of us is susceptible to the perceptions and judgments imposed upon us by external sources. Projection occurs when an individual holds certain beliefs or emotions about themselves and consequently assumes that these traits or sentiments are common among all others. They begin to perceive that those surrounding them are, in fact, exhibiting a certain characteristic or habit that aligns with their own. Individuals tend to categorize others and impose predetermined behavioral expectations upon them. It is imperative

that you grant yourself the liberty to unequivocally dismiss their notions pertaining to your being. Refuse to succumb to their efforts to confine you within predetermined boundaries.

Provide yourself with positive affirmation

A crucial aspect of effectively countering Dark Persuasion is cultivating the ability to comprehend the malevolent forces in play and consciously exposing oneself to contradictory information. Gaining comprehension of Dark Psychology entails willingly immersing oneself to some extent in the realm of darkness. Nevertheless, after undertaking this action, it will be necessary to harmonize your energy by incorporating optimistic thoughts into your mindset. By offering oneself optimistic affirmations in order to counterbalance the presence of negative influences, one will discover the capacity to prevail over any forms of manipulation or deceit.

Exhibit authenticity regarding your accomplishments

Don't be humble. Certainly, displaying humility is commendable, albeit within certain limits. The embrace of modesty will ultimately culminate in your downfall. Align yourself with the views of Machiavelli on this particular matter and grant yourself the ability to wholeheartedly commend your own achievements. Individualism is a fundamental principle deeply rooted in Western culture, characterized by the wholehearted acceptance of one's own identity, desires, and lifestyle. Celebrate yourself. Convince yourself that you are entitled to success. Adopt a realistic assessment of your existing achievements – it is highly probable that you have made significant progress.

Envision your future

Embrace a courageous approach to your future. If one consistently harbors a vision of a forthcoming characterized by distress and agony, it is highly likely that one's efforts will be directed towards its materialization. If you have the capacity to conceive a prospective outcome for yourself characterized by accomplishment and supremacy, you will significantly enhance your chances of manifesting it in actuality.

Identify and acknowledge your personal areas for improvement in order to effectively address them.

Your unconscious mind has the propensity to deceive and mislead. On occasion, it may lead you to believe that you are flawless and devoid of imperfections, despite this being an inaccurate perception. The majority of individuals possess one or two areas in which they can make improvements. If you can identify these aspects within yourself, you will discover the capacity to align more closely with the journey of self-realization.

Embrace gratitude

Cultivating an attitude of gratitude entails nurturing a positive self-perception, which will facilitate your journey toward self-actualization. Certain individuals have experienced harm to their subconscious, resulting in feelings of bitterness and diminished resilience due to previous adversities. It is imperative that you acquire the ability to refrain from succumbing to such inclinations, and it is equally essential that you discover a sense of appreciation for the world around you. This will enhance the resilience of your defenses while imparting the valuable lesson that certain endeavors hold merit in fostering your pursuit of happiness.

Determine your desired objectives, and acquire them.

Cease engaging in frivolous behavior and impeding your own progress towards obtaining your desires. If you lack knowledge on acquiring it, then make an effort to gain the skills necessary to obtain it. If your objective is to pursue a specific professional trajectory, consider inquiring about the possibility of becoming an apprentice under someone's tutelage. If the matter is within the realm of self-acquisition, conduct thorough research and commence the process of independently acquiring the necessary knowledge and skills to accomplish the desired outcome. Engage in extensive reading, utilize online resources, and seek insights from individuals who have successfully attained your desired goals.

Detach yourself from your fixation on the methodology.

The method employed holds no significance. The means by which one seeks to attain their desires and necessities pose a significant obstacle. This is the juncture where discernment becomes crucial. The subconscious mind may occasionally propel one towards forming judgments, and it can be observed that the presence of an inner voice that encourages judgment tends to introduce a discernable gap between one's desires and current circumstances. It is advisable that you endeavor to minimize this gap to the greatest extent possible.

Chapter Six: The Power of Subtle Influence

D

Coercive manipulation encompasses various methodologies that are consistently employed to influence individuals into reducing their cognitive capacities, thus compelling compliance with prescribed directives. Neuro-linguistic programming (NLP) encompasses a singular facet of engaging with one's own thoughts and behaviors, as well as the thoughts and behaviors of others, with the aim of acquiring discernment, resilience, and safeguards against exploitation by malevolent individuals. This chapter shall provide an in-depth explanation of NLP and proffer recommendations on incorporating the principles of this methodology to enhance your personal growth and progress.

This chapter shall additionally impart knowledge on revealing the concealed persuader, dissecting the conveyed messages, and establishing a mental distance between oneself and the subconscious mind. By doing so, one can effectively process communication and enhance overall functionality in various aspects of life. A significant number of individuals succumb to the traps inherent in the persuasive messages bombarding them from various directions.

Methods of employing subtle influence encompass brainwashing, deceit, discreet manipulation, and various other facets of communication and duplicity. By learning to analyze what you read, hear, and learn, you will start to be able to delineate what is good for you, what is honest, and who is lying. Commence acquiring the skills to counteract negative influence and enhance your personal success.

There are many psychological factors that go into the process of covert manipulation and dark persuasion. Some of these include psychological vulnerability, self-awareness, confidence, trust, and the capacity to evaluate others. If you enhance your abilities in these domains, you will acquire the capacity to comprehend the ways in which you have been subjected to manipulation in the past, and to steer clear of such circumstances in the future. Throughout history, monarchs and leaders have employed manipulation and persuasion as means to acquire and consolidate their authority. Power is attained by individuals who possess the capacity to employ their intellect independently from the emotional distractions and trivialities that commonly preoccupy the general public. The objective is not to relinquish emotions and adopt a detached demeanor, but rather to cultivate an awareness of how to navigate existence with a resolute sense of personal identity, assurance, and unwavering resolve that will enable you to achieve desired outcomes.

This chapter additionally examines the concept of self-actualization, strategies for circumventing persuasion, the subconscious mind, and their correlation with comprehending the manipulative aspects of deception and psychological manipulation. The journey of personal growth is a challenging one, yet this section will facilitate your journey towards gaining a comprehensive awareness of your aptitudes and limitations. Armed with this knowledge, you will be empowered to confront the adversities that hinder your progress.

If you desire to acquire the knowledge of effectively influencing someone's decisions without causing annoyance, it is imperative to familiarize yourself with the techniques of persuasion. If one is able to acquire proficiency in these techniques, one will readily possess the ability to convince individuals to comply with one's desires without being perceived as bothersome. These techniques encompass a spectrum, ranging from possessing a thorough understanding of the subject matter to being perceived as a person of authority. If you desire to acquire knowledge regarding the art of convincing individuals to engage in actions without causing any annoyance, it is imperative that you possess a comprehensive understanding of the subject matter being communicated. It is imperative to ensure the accuracy of your information, maintain logical reasoning, and be sufficiently prepared to counter any arguments raised by your opponent. You risk cultivating an impression of being bothersome rather than influential if it fails to appear that your statements lack substance.

Be cheerful and polite. Make an effort to charm the individual you are endeavoring to persuade. Individuals are more inclined to heed the words of an individual who assumes a leadership role as opposed to one who adopts a follower position. Exhibit leadership qualities and you will be perceived as significantly more influential to individuals in your vicinity. Individuals typically possess an inclination towards acquiring new knowledge; however, they tend to scrutinize its credibility by assessing the credibility of the source presenting the information.

One of the fundamental aspects in acquiring the skill of persuading individuals without causing annoyance is to ensure that one refrains from pestering them. You will be regarded as more persuasive if you avoid appearing excessively exertive in your attempts to convince them to engage in the desired action.

Exhibit patience and respectfully request that they contemplate undertaking the task, allowing them ample time for deliberation. Requesting them to immediately perform that particular task may not always be the most optimal course of action. A significant number of individuals will persistently decline in order to avoid conceding the argument at hand. Provide a thorough explanation of your rationale and subsequently allow them sufficient time. They may eventually choose to undertake it of their own volition.

The aforementioned strategies represent only a subset of the methodologies one can utilize to exert influence over others in a manner that avoids causing any undue irritation. There is a wide range of approaches at your disposal to gain extensive understanding of how to successfully convince individuals to conform to your desired actions, while concurrently ensuring minimal disturbance and preventing the development of any hostility towards your objectives. A skilled influencer will employ diverse strategies, including nonverbal signals and even the usage of hypnosis. One salient feature is that these techniques are accessible to individuals from all backgrounds. Should you wish to attain information on the matter, I kindly advise consulting the suggested resource that has been consequently offered.

Gaining a comprehensive comprehension of the art of persuasion is the sole requirement to exert a compelling influence on individuals. Upon attaining proficiency in the art of persuasion, my entire existence underwent a remarkable metamorphosis for the better. I was presented with an opportunity for career advancement and was appreciating acknowledgement for the significance of my contributions. I am no anomaly, and you possess the capacity to accomplish the same.

Persuasion Everywhere

Allow us to first address the misconception that covert persuasion is difficult to attain. Take note of your environment and you will notice that it is omnipresent, although a significant number of individuals remain unaware of its existence on a daily basis.

Have you ever opted for one brand of beer over another based on a commercial advertisement? You might not be cognizant of this fact, but the brewers allocate significant monetary resources every year to ensure that this conviction becomes ingrained in you.

Have you ever come across an individual with whom you instantly felt a profound sense of resonance? The impact of their body language on it may have been unintentional, irrespective of their intentions, as opposed to ascribing it solely to your intuition.

The Profound Benefits of Concealed Hypnosis for Individuals of All Walks of Life

What is the fundamental drive behind influencing individuals? Each interpersonal exchange we partake in, apart from those involving close associates and relatives, usually entails a pursuit of mutual agreement. From time to time, a situation may arise wherein you may achieve success in certain circumstances, while encountering failure in others.

Imagine the remarkable accomplishments one can achieve in life through the acquisition of knowledge and skills that consistently allow one to secure a position of advantage - thereby enabling increased financial remuneration, the ability to negotiate more favorable terms for goods or services, captivating the affection of a desired individual, facilitating consensus during meetings, and attaining various other significant triumphs.

Utilization of Manual Gestures as an Exemplary Technique

Gestures made with the hands can function as a highly effective method of subtly exerting influence over individuals. Most individuals commonly utilize hand gestures during communication, however, the recipient seldom focuses their attention on the gestures themselves. This provides an opportunity to integrate instructions and subtly suggest concepts.

For example, in the context of a job interview, it can be beneficial to adeptly showcase to individuals with vested interests that you are the most fitting applicant for the position. First and foremost, it is critical to determine the interviewer's unfavorable disposition. When individuals participate in unfavorable conversations, they typically express a singular inclination, either towards the left or the right.

Consequently, when discussing commendable individuals, including oneself, it is appropriate to acknowledge oneself. When addressing individuals who might have lower skills or any deficiencies, it is recommended to

imitate the actions displayed by the interviewer.
This is an exceedingly efficacious technique that yields excellent results.

Securing the Long-Term Integration of the New Ideology

When endeavoring to modify one's beliefs, it is imperative to ascertain that the new conviction authentically aligns with the ideal individual one aspires to embody. It is imperative to uphold a profound sense of personal integrity throughout this phase, as choices influenced by self-deception are rarely sustainable in the long term. Understanding the deep-seated reasoning behind implementing a change is just as essential in fully embracing and incorporating it into our practices. The phrase utilized to elucidate the procedure of ensuring concordance between the novel conviction and an individual's value system is commonly known as an ecological evaluation.

The ecological assessment may encompass a spectrum of approaches, varying from a straightforward process to a more comprehensive undertaking that entails meticulous examination. A newly acquired belief may naturally align with reason and require minimal effort for its seamless incorporation into your everyday life. However, it may also be imperative to verify the accuracy of the information. You may find it imperative to conduct introspection through a succession of interrogations. Does this align with my emotional preferences? What are the potential advantages that can be attained from embracing this newfound belief system? Does this newfound belief have a substantial enough influence to warrant my complete commitment, despite any temptations to return to my previous conviction? Does this align with my ethical principles? What are the expenses related to this alteration, and am I sufficiently equipped to assume them?

Consider this thorough ecological analysis as a crucial measure in transforming your perspective on life. It functions as a mechanism for assessing the integrity of your intentions, and ensures that once you make a pledge, there are no conceivable reasons for its foreseeable downfall. You have conducted extensive and meticulous research beforehand, thereby indicating that the achievement of positive outcomes from your newfound conviction is the only viable outcome.

V - Anticipatory Encouragement

Setting goals and achieving them are separate endeavors, and a significant challenge arises from our ability to appropriately prepare ourselves for the path towards success. However, another facet of the challenge resides in our capacity to nurture the essential qualities and characteristics needed to achieve the goals we have established for ourselves. Numerous individuals who have attained noteworthy accomplishments frequently articulate that the most gratifying element of their endeavor towards objectives resides in observing the personal maturation and advancement that transpires throughout the course. It would be advisable to give precedence to the planning and preparedness required for undertaking such a transformative endeavor.

When we set forth formidable and ambitious goals, it becomes effortless to envision the obstacles that await us on our journey. We might unintentionally become absorbed in imagining a harmful interaction.

That composition will present itself as arduous to produce.

It seems extremely unlikely to partake in strenuous physical activity consistently over a duration of six months.

The anticipated project schedule is expected to evoke considerable frustration and present notable challenges for me.

In addition, it is just as effortless to disregard the significance of adequately defining those obstacles and participating in deliberate mental readiness to surmount them. Furthermore, we frequently fail to sufficiently equip ourselves for unforeseen eventualities that may emerge throughout our expedition. However, akin to the rigorous practice undertaken by athletes in preparation for a championship game, we can utilize the principles of neurolinguistic programming to effectively equip ourselves for success as we strive towards our ambitious goals.

Multiple scholarly researches have consistently revealed that the observation of one athlete performing a physical action triggers neuromuscular activities in the observer, replicating the electromyographic responses that would typically occur during the actual execution of the same movement. Similarly, when an athlete engages in the act of envisioning the execution of a particular motion, they experience authentic impulses. Remember the mirror neurons? Certainly, these factors are at play within this particular context, and we possess the ability to utilize them to our advantage. In a manner akin to how a sportsman utilizes the strategy of mentally envisioning an ideal performance to boost the probability of attaining their objectives, we also have the ability to embrace and incorporate this method.

First and foremost, it is imperative to foster an expectation of a positive outcome throughout the course of our undertaking. This objective can be attained by employing techniques such as utilizing affirmative self-affirmations, engaging in introspective writing exercises, or employing imaginative imagery. The incorporation of diverse methodologies leads to more resilient conclusions.

Regardless of the methodology employed, the primary aim persists in establishing a benchmark for success, satisfaction, and fulfillment in all our undertakings. Effectively harnessing language and emotions is integral and necessitates careful strategic implementation for optimal advantage. For example, when engaging in the technique of creating affirmations, it is crucial to utilize powerful resources at our disposal, such as employing terms like "effortlessly" and "with the utmost ease." The deliberate selection of these words serves to magnify a feeling of favorable interaction and participation. I possess a strong belief in my ability to secure a position in the upper echelon of my company's worldwide stack rankings for the ongoing quarter. My resolute objective is to achieve a weight reduction of ten pounds within the forthcoming three-month period.

Embarking upon the endeavor with a clear vision of the ultimate objective, while maintaining the belief that it will yield favorable outcomes, profoundly influences the cultivation of a resolute mentality that is steadfast until the culmination. When creating abstract representations of achievement, give precedence to enhancing the profound emotions linked with happiness, success, and fulfillment. Permit these emotions to function as a guiding force, directing you towards the ultimate reward that awaits you upon reaching the conclusion of your journey.

The preliminary stage bears immense importance in laying the foundation for success; nevertheless, subsequent to the establishment of the groundwork, it remains essential for us to fully grasp the strategy we will adopt to accomplish this goal. The route that connects Point A and Point B is distinguished by a serpentine trajectory replete with impediments and tumult. There is no reason to be alarmed, and these circumstances do not present a risk to our achievements, as long as we sufficiently ready ourselves, similar to how athletes diligently train to effectively face strong opponents. Nevertheless, disregarding the preparation and practice required for managing these obstacles is akin to presuming that you will be the sole contender vying for a promotion. It can be likened to devising a strategic plan to ensure the sole presence of our team on the football field. Engaging in such behavior positions oneself for eventual failure.

The premature relinquishment of one's goals frequently arises from insufficient readiness to embark upon the journey of attaining them. A committed learner whose primary objective is to achieve an impeccable 4.0 GPA can find themselves teetering on the edge of failure when faced with their first significant task, grappling with mounting obligations and an immense sense of pressure. Why? As a consequence of his exclusive focus on completing the mentioned assignment as documented in his academic record, he failed to adhere to the disciplined practice of attending regular classes during a period of sixteen weeks, engaging in collaborative study sessions, and dedicating hours to working on academic papers during nighttime. He was caught off guard by the unforeseen challenges, and he had not adequately made arrangements to effectively tackle them.

On the other hand, a manager who is preparing to interview for a role in the executive leadership team of her organization could begin by envisioning herself seated behind the desk embellished with a maple finish in her potential corner office. In addition, she has anticipated the need for thorough practice sessions that will be necessary in the upcoming month to sufficiently prepare her presentation for the Board. Upon taking her place in the interview room, she envisions her heart throbbing with zealousness. Upon acknowledging the interviewers and adapting to her surroundings, she has become aware of the peaceful atmosphere that surrounds her. She has envisioned the interviewers asking a question for which she lacks preparation, the way in which she gracefully acknowledges their inquiry as a strategy to buy time for contemplation, and her proficiency in expressing her ideas and delivering a convincing response. She has anticipated the upcoming phase subsequent to the interview, during which she encounters varying degrees of uncertainty and apprehension. She has contemplated the situation in which, during a Tuesday morning, she examines her email inbox and encounters a job offer letter directed to her from the highly regarded Chairman.

Strategic planning for facilitating extraordinary life transformations.

Traditional Goal Setting

To commence advancement, it is crucial to possess a comprehensive comprehension of the intended endpoint. It is not feasible for an individual to embark upon an exploration of the extensive domain of the world without due deliberation and anticipate fortuitously reaching a significantly advantageous outcome, as it is commonly acknowledged that life does not conform to such elementary principles. During the course of your expedition, it is possible that you may encounter something truly enchanting, invoking a sense of wonder that propels you to embark upon its pursuit. What is the likelihood of this event transpiring? It is highly likely that you will wander without clear direction for a specific duration, resulting in the eventual culmination of your endeavors. And as a result, you will inevitably find yourself confiding in the depths of your own moral compass:

I observe a lack of achievements in the path I have taken in my life. I anticipate an enduring pattern of repeated failures persisting to dominate my trajectory. What obstacles hinder my ability to attain the level of success that others have accomplished?

The list could perpetually continue, without interruption.

Nevertheless, it is crucial to acknowledge that should individuals persist in passively conforming to the predestined trajectory of their existence, none of these aspirations will come to fruition. It is of utmost importance that you take charge and mold your life in accordance with your desired aspirations. Defining goals will aid you in achieving this result.

Allow me to clarify, I am not alluding to the conventional method of establishing goals where one merely envisions different aspirations without a tangible plan or strategic framework for their achievement. The methodology employed for goal setting through the application of NLP varies, and the rationales underlying this differentiation will be expounded upon in the following sections.

When engaging with a self-help or productivity manual, and being enlightened about the importance of setting goals, a large number of individuals tend to view matters in a simplistic or limited way. We may endeavor to optimize our efficiency, augment our fiscal resources, cultivate romantic partnerships, overcome social inhibitions, or pursue any other aspirations we may have. Our deficiency can be attributed to our limited capability in efficiently achieving these objectives.

We meticulously record and transcribe the information onto a physical medium, harboring a positive outlook in terms of its eventual realization. Certainly, we have diligently exerted ourselves, have we not? The outstanding tasks should be relatively simple to complete. Wrong!

You will be pleased to discover that you are on the brink of acquiring the utmost effective and focused strategy for goal-setting that you have ever come across. Additionally, it is crucial to acknowledge that these aims should not be formulated solely on societal norms, but rather derived from genuine internal aspirations that hold profound significance to your essence. Are you ready to determine the approach? Here goes:

Goal Setting NLP-Style

Before embarking on the process of setting our remarkable life goals, let us take a moment to consider how goal setting with NLP is demonstrated.

The ensuing actions will assist you in devising profoundly impactful goals.

Understand the fundamental justification behind setting objectives. You are not simply setting a random goal; instead, you are undertaking the task of developing a thorough strategy to attain exceptional results. You are approaching the point of envisioning an enhanced way of life, you are at the threshold of crafting a compelling vision that harmonizes with your ambitions.

Dream without limits

It commences with the ambitions you possess. Regrettably, a significant portion of individuals has unfortunately lost the ability to imagine, due to the misconception that aspirations rarely materialize.

Your statement is highly erroneous.

To translate your aspirations into tangible achievements, it is crucial that you allow yourself to envision and wholeheartedly embrace your dreams with the same wonder and imagination as a child.

Kindly devote some time to visualizing the attributes of your envisioned life.

In the context of an optimal way of living, which daily pursuits would you partake in? What type of breakfast would you typically partake in? What is your intended distribution of time between your professional pursuits and leisurely pursuits? Among the various passions available, which one would you opt to earnestly pursue? To whose company do you aspire to surround yourself with?

Examine yourself through these inquiries and challenge the undermining beliefs of uncertainty, including the idea that "it will never materialize."

Engaging in imaginative thinking is not limited to conforming to the bounds of reality; instead, it involves bestowing upon oneself the liberty to construct an alternative realm within the realm of one's own mind.

You are strongly encouraged to contemplate potentialities that may presently appear to transcend the boundaries of what is realistic.

Rather than becoming excessively focused on the methods, shift your focus towards the ultimate goal.

If you are encountering challenges in doing so, partake in the subsequent activity: make an earnest effort to imaginatively depict a situation in which you have recently obtained a considerable amount of wealth, totaling millions of dollars. What is the proposed plan for the allocation of the available funds? What is your ultimate purpose or ambition in determining the allocation of your entire life? Which type of lifestyle would you opt to embrace?

Partake in introspective analysis and uphold honesty in your process of self-evaluation. There is no compulsion to reveal your aspirations to others; engage in this exercise exclusively for your personal advantage. Refrain from self-deception and demonstrate the boldness to once more engage in imaginative pursuits.

What are your earnest ambitions? There is no inherently correct or incorrect response; it would be prudent to stay true to your own set of principles and convictions.

Dream in 3D

It is anticipated that you have articulated certain aspirations at this juncture. Suppose these were

▫ Travel the world

▫ Find a girlfriend/boyfriend

Do not allow these ambitions to persist as remote possibilities with a slim chance of being realized.

I would appreciate it if you could take a moment to gently lower your eyelids and employ your creative faculties to envision yourself participating in all the activities that you yearn for.

Imagine yourself undertaking a worldwide expedition, embracing the challenge of scaling Mount Everest, navigating through the vastness of the Amazon, or pursuing any ambition that holds significance for you. Envision yourself leisurely walking alongside your esteemed companion. Take note of the complete presentation in vibrant Technicolor and bear witness to its dynamic animation.

Observe the vibrant colors in which your aspirations come to life, as the overwhelming feeling of turning your dreams into reality permeates your mind. Witness the realization of your aspirations.

Conceive a vivid and comprehensive portrayal of your aspirations and ambitions, enabling your thoughts to explore the highest level of detail attainable.

Participating in this endeavor will provide you with the opportunity to firmly establish your aspirations, clarify their details, and ultimately increase the likelihood of achieving them.

Design Your Action Plan

Define Obstacles

After establishing the intended destination, it is crucial to formulate a suitable plan of action that will enable the achievement of the objective.

Therefore, opt for this unique and substantial aspiration.

Initially, it is crucial to carefully consider the obstacles that must be overcome in order to achieve this goal.

Some possible factors include limitations in financial resources, reduced confidence, mental health conditions such as social anxiety disorders, impaired self-esteem, and comparable concerns.

I kindly implore you to consider the challenges that may impede your progress in the pursuit of your desired goal. By utilizing Natural Language Processing (NLP) techniques, you will gain the requisite knowledge and competencies to effectively address the aforementioned challenges, subsequently converting them into strategic advantages in the subsequent sections.

Now that we have identified all the main obstacles, we will now move forward with developing a comprehensive strategy for each specific challenge, following a methodical approach.

Have a Step-by-Step Plan

Clarify your priorities.

Prioritizing the resolution of your lack of self-assurance would be prudent before embarking on any future pursuits, such as seeking a salary raise, transitioning careers, or undertaking any other endeavors."

Which task will you give precedence to at the outset? What specific responsibilities, obstacles, and adaptations will be expected of you in the forthcoming period? What is the main obstacle that you must overcome in order to proceed?

It is recommended that you methodically recognize and evaluate all obstacles, and devise a comprehensive range of tactics to surmount any barriers that may obstruct the achievement of your goals.

The implementation of your proposed strategy requires breaking down each obstacle into smaller, sequential tasks.

Set SMART goals

To ensure the realization of your aspirations, it is crucial to set forth precise objectives. The absence of precise details will inevitably impede your advancement. In order to achieve goals with optimal effectiveness, I strongly recommend the implementation of S.M.A.R.T objective-setting methodologies. By embracing this methodology, you can establish a meticulously crafted and refined tactic that will amplify your comprehension of your goals, empowering you to make expeditious and effective strides towards their achievement. Permit me to provide a comprehensive explanation of the sequential procedures required to achieve this objective.

May I kindly request an elucidation on the concept of S.M.A.R.T goals at the outset?

S.M.A.R.T is an initialism that encapsulates the tenets of being Specific, Measurable, Achievable, Realistic, and Time-bound.

Specific:

By defining a specific goal, you enhance the probability of accomplishing it effectively.

Reflect upon a cherished ambition; engage in self-inquiry pertaining to the following six queries commencing with the letter "W":

Regarding whom are the individuals in question engaged?

What is the intended outcome I am striving to achieve?

Where: Find a location.

When considering the timing, establish the chronological parameters.

Kindly analyze and articulate the precise array of prerequisites and limitations pertaining to the provided scenario.

The rationales, objectives, or advantages driving the accomplishment of the goal.

To provide an example, let us contemplate the theoretical endeavor of "embarking on voyages across various regions of the world." This objective is lacking in clarity and necessitates additional specification. It would be more appropriate to articulate it in the following manner: "My objective is to acquire a ticket to Paris and coordinate lodging for a week-long sojourn alongside my spouse, commencing on August 1st and concluding on August 8th."

Measurable

It is crucial to develop a method for assessing your progress towards your goal to safeguard against feelings of discouragement during periods of difficulty. Once a method of measuring it has been established, there is an increased likelihood of sustaining concentration and achieving the intended outcome. In order to evaluate the achievability of your objective, establish a set of benchmarks to address the question: what indicators will signify its attainment? Through which criteria can one conclusively determine if my objective has been achieved?

Attainable

Certain aspirations you may have may currently be unattainable or lie beyond your reach in the foreseeable future. However, it is imperative to note that such circumstances are completely acceptable.

Hence, it is imperative to establish which dreams can be further broken down into more feasible goals that retain their significance to you, while being less arduous to achieve.

Allow us to ponder the scenario of undertaking a worldwide expedition. It is possible that your existing financial circumstances may prevent you from undertaking any travels at this time. One alternative phrasing in a more formal tone might be: "In order to make progress toward your noteworthy ambition, it is advisable to undertake a comprehensive financial evaluation to ascertain the necessary investment. Following this, you can proceed to determine strategies for minimizing expenses." This could involve a thorough examination of your budget or investigating possible options for generating supplementary income. Participating in a constructive dialogue with your spouse regarding your plans may serve as an supplementary step. Moreover, the inclusion of various examples or instances may be continual and appear limitless.

The pursuit of any course of action will serve as an essential element of a comprehensive strategy designed to attain the overarching vision you hold.

If a goal seems inaccessible at this point in time, it might be prudent to set a more realistic target. This goal should be readily achievable, requiring only a minimal amount of effort.

The act of formulating goals will consistently remain a continuous endeavor. As individuals make headway in achieving smaller milestones, goals that were formerly perceived as remote will gradually approach and transform into attainable accomplishments. This phenomenon manifests itself when the attainment of minor objectives triggers a process of individual metamorphosis, marked by enhanced personal development, the broadening of skills, and the amelioration of circumstances.

Realistic

A matter that requires your deliberation is: do I possess the capacity to achieve the goal I have recently set for myself? Is it conceivable from my vantage point?

To ensure a practical standpoint, it is essential that a goal is a feasible objective requiring your dedication and ability to actively pursue. It is ultimately your responsibility to assess the appropriate scope of your ambitions and evaluate their feasibility.

It would be prudent for you to develop your beliefs by actively integrating a constructive belief framework. Given a sincere belief in the feasibility of your goal, it is possible to accomplish it. Alternative ways to determine the attainability of your goal encompass assessing prior instances in which you successfully accomplished a similar undertaking, or contemplating the necessary factors that must be in place to achieve such an objective.

If you have not yet accomplished similar goals, instead of dwelling on the unlikelihood of achieving this new goal, consider other potential routes; prompt your mind to be open to suggestions; undertake thorough research on strategies to attain your objective.

Exercise 9: Compulsion Killer

Do you face challenges in abstaining from negative habits, such as indulging in tobacco or alcohol consumption, or engaging in nail-biting? Would it not be advantageous to possess a convenient and straightforward exercise at your disposal, serving as a means to surmount the impulses driving you towards engaging in compulsive behavior? Engage in this NLP exercise as a means to effectively overcome your cravings.

Commence by evoking in your thoughts the object or conduct that you yearn for, or encounter difficulty in refraining from. Consider, for example, the scenario where you aim to break the habit of consuming an excessive amount of chocolate. In this exercise, it is advisable to conjure an image of your preferred chocolate bar.

Please take a moment to carefully contemplate and observe this vivid mental representation within the depths of your imagination. Please make a careful observation of the attributes of this image. How large is it? How colorful is it? Do you perceive it as being in proximity to you, or at a considerable distance? Is the clarity of this image satisfactory? Is there a border present? Do not overly ponder upon the responses to these inquiries; instead, rely on your innate intuition. Note them down.

The subsequent action entails conjuring a neutral visual representation. For example, consider the scenario where you find it challenging to resist consuming chocolate, but you remain completely unaffected by cigarettes. In this case, you can visualize a mental representation of a cigarette during this segment of the activity. Once more, please take note of the subsequent characteristics associated with this cognitive representation: its dimensions, its hue, its spatial location, and the additional factors delineated in the preceding paragraph. You may likely observe variations in the characteristics of your compulsive and non-compulsive images across these dimensions.

Following your analysis of the compulsive and non-compulsive images, it is now incumbent upon you to undertake a cognitive exploration, considering the pertinent factors, in order to diminish the grip of the compulsive image on your mind. For instance, it is evident that the dimensions of the cognitive representation linked to the chocolate bar (the compulsive image) are substantially greater and more distinct compared to the cognitive representation associated with the cigarette (the non-compulsive image). To mitigate the compulsion, one could amplify the size and vibrant hues to an extent that it becomes mentally overpowering and entirely devoid of attraction. On each instance that the compulsive image is encountered, it is advised to mentally amplify it, imbuing it with vivid hues so vibrant that it forfeits all significance and assumes a highly farcical nature. If you were to engage in this practice multiple times, you may discover that your previously compelling images no longer evoke the same level of compulsion.

What is the correlation between depression and NLP?

Prior to initiating our exploration of various learning techniques, let us first inquire about the essence of NLP.

NPL is an acronym that represents the term Neuro Linguistic Programming. This approach pertains to the acquisition of knowledge related to cognitive thinking and information processing. This system possesses the capability to modify an individual's behavior by equipping them with the necessary techniques to effectively manage any situation, whether it involves negative thought patterns or feelings of depression and guilt. Because of this, people can cope with these situations in a more positive way so that they are able to bounce back quicker than they used to.

During the early 1970s, Richard Bandler and John Grinder, an accomplished mathematician and linguist respectively, united their expertise in pursuit of understanding the circumstances that led individuals to demonstrate competence in a specific domain, surpassing their peers in this regard.

Thanks to the advancements in NLP, it has been revealed that altering one's thought patterns, in conjunction with the use of positive language, has the ability to modify an individual's behavior. NLP empowers individuals to modify, adjust, or eliminate behaviors that may be detrimental to their well-being. Engaging in this endeavor facilitates the refinement of individuals' aptitude whilst fostering personal growth arising from the diverse array of life situations encountered. NLP provides a distinct array of mechanisms designed to enhance individuals' overall well-being and foster cognitive advancement.

The brain is a highly intricate organ, however, we are capable of comprehending the thought processes of individuals. This understanding, in turn, serves to enhance our life experiences and alter our responses to stimuli that would typically elicit negative reactions. Various methodologies exist to facilitate an individual's comprehension and perception of the world from an alternative perspective. Nevertheless, given our tendency to be resistant to change, altering the functioning of our mind can occasionally elicit an adverse response. In the majority of instances, it will afford us the ability to modify our way of managing adverse encounters.

There exists a proverb that goes as follows: "Continuously engaging in the same actions will yield the same results indefinitely." Nevertheless, the field of Neuro-Linguistic Programming (NLP) challenges this notion, as it posits that the neural reactions to pessimistic thoughts will undergo a transformation. The adverse reaction towards life events arises when individuals perceive a lack of alternative approaches to cope with the current circumstances.

Not only will the application of these techniques facilitate your management of depression, but they will also empower you to effectively handle any adversarial emotions that manifest. Simply direct your attention towards a novel emotion while employing that particular strategy for an alternative purpose.

Depression frequently entails experiencing a profound sense of despair and a lack of confidence in the positive outcomes of one's life circumstances. It engenders an overwhelming sense of despair that permeates your being, engulfing you in a state of uncertainty concerning your ability to escape it.

Nevertheless, the application of NLP techniques can assist you in managing your depression or any other adverse emotions you might be experiencing, thereby augmenting both the frequency and intensity of your feelings of happiness.

Please refrain from anticipating immediate effectiveness of these approaches. You are going to have to practice to get them to work for you. Moreover, it is plausible that there may not be efficacious strategies at your disposal. If such strategies prove to be futile, there is no necessity for you to persist in futile attempts to make them operative. If you discover a solution that proves effective, proceed with that approach; in the event it fails, discontinue and transition to an alternative method.

There will be occasions where a blend of methodologies will prove effective, and such instances are completely acceptable. The opinions and comments of others are inconsequential; it is imperative that you prioritize your own well-being in order to effectively address the depression you are experiencing.

Your depression is not an eternal affliction; rest assured, you will acquire the resilience to manage it and lead a fulfilling life.

Persist in searching for the illumination that lies beyond adversity, so as to perpetuate your onward progression. Although you may currently be experiencing a sense of darkness, be assured that there is a light on the horizon which will ultimately illuminate your path and lead to a positive resolution.

www.ingramcontent.com/pod-product-compliance
Lightning Source LLC
Chambersburg PA
CBHW050243120526
44590CB00016B/2197